Introduction

You feel like there's something missing from your life as a Christian and you want to do something about it. There seem to be people around you who have got the whole Holy Spirit thing figured out - they don't have it all figured out, by the way. FOMO (fear of missing out) kicks and you want to discover and experience more of the full life as a disciple of Christ. Where do you turn? What resources are available for you to begin intentionally try to grow and mature as a believer? Your first go-to must be your local pastor. Someone who knows you, loves you, and accepts you as a fellow disciple of Christ. There are many resources for your pastor and/ or counselor to recommend.

This companion journal is a guided internal discussion to help with intentional followership. If you came to this book seeking answers to specific questions you may be disappointed. The Waypoint Chronicles series poses questions to enable you to process issues intentionally. When a topic needs further explanation, seek out your local pastor or counselor. I believe that knowledge is a commodity that is easily obtained in our online, AI driven world. The more difficult and relevant part lies in knowing the questions that need asking and answered personally by you as an individual. You will discover new avenues of communication with the Holy Spirit and fellow believers as you move through this book.

If you are not yet a disciple of Christ, you may find this to be a stretch. That's OK, we're glad you're attempting to heal and change your life. But this is written with the assumption that you are a faithful follower of Christ and have a local church that you are active in. Local church fellowship and friendship is a valuable resource and significant support in troubled times.

Although this workbook is designed for you to write in and keep, we also suggest maintaining a separate logbook or journal to document your progress. Yes, that's a lot of writing and time but your life as a disciple of Christ is worth it. And more importantly, your discipleship journey with Christ is a worthy pursuit in ways we can never imagine when we take it seriously.

The wind blows where it wishes, and you hear its sound, but you do not know where it comes from or where it goes. So it is with everyone who is born of the Spirit.

John 3:8 (ESV)

Accepting responsibility for your own actions and attitudes is contrary to the way many of us live our lives. We like to play the blame game by shifting responsibility or blame to other people. I was a military weather forecaster for many years and trained many new forecasters. It was always the case, without exception that I can recall, that the new person would use the phrase "they said/say" regarding the forecast he or she was giving. When I pressed them into why they used that phrase, sometimes it was because they were shifting responsibility to another forecaster, but most of the time, it was a nebulous reference to a computer-generated model. The question I then asked was, "who is signing the DD175-1" (the weather forecast form given for every military flight mission)? Since the forecaster signed the form, no one else could be held responsible for the information the forecaster was sharing. He or she had to take responsibility for the information being disseminated.

The shifts and blame are often so subtle no one notices, even the person communicating. True discipleship does not allow for overt or covert blame-shifting. We cannot make excuses for not following the Holy Spirit. We must take full responsibility for our actions and attitudes as we sail the open waters of life.

To be guided effectively by the Holy Spirit, you need to accept who you are in Him. You must be prepared to live differently than non-believers and casual Christians live. Being fully guided by the Holy Spirit is very comforting, yet unbelievably difficult, if not impossible, to be grasped by anyone not fully submitted to Him. Living your life by navigating the open waters of life by the Holy Spirit is an exciting and rewarding experience. It means that you're taking a unique path and allowing God to create a life for you that no one else has lived before. It can be a bit scary at first, as you have to figure out your way of navigating the unknown. But as you look back on your journey, you can be proud of yourself for taking the risk and embracing the journey God has for you and you alone. You'll learn new skills and gain confidence in your ability to make the right decisions. You'll also get to explore new places, meet interesting people, and learn valuable lessons along the way. These experiences will enrich your life and make you a more well-rounded person. So, don't be afraid to take the plunge and set sail on your journey. You will find adventure and fulfillment if you do.

As a devoted disciple of Christ, I need to accept that I will never be fully mature on this side of heaven. But I do have a responsibility to continue to grow as a disciple of Christ. I've always been a big-picture, visually oriented learner. I like to see how what I am doing fits into the bigger picture with the task, project, or life situation I find myself in.

Early on as a disciple of Christ, this way of thinking led to a desire to be someone God didn't create for me to be and led me down the wrong path. In seeking discipleship growth, I tried following people whom I admired in their Christian journey by mimicking what I saw them doing. Other times, I thought growth might come through climbing a spiritual ladder of sorts by progressing to more "in-depth" study and discovery. Ultimately, I actively searched and prayed that God would reveal what it means to be a growing, maturing Christian. The picture God clearly placed in me was that of a sailboat on the open ocean, with the sails billowing with the wind.

Our lives are not to be lived on a path trod by someone else or on a preset map already navigated. We are to hoist the sail and follow the Holy Spirit's design for our life lives on the open waters of life. We are often tempted to grab the rudder and impede the work of the Holy Spirit by tacking in a direction He didn't intend. If we simply allow Him to guide us in making small rudder corrections with the wind of the Holy Spirit, our journey will be smooth and not shifting rapidly to and fro. Staying on His course does not forgo rough waters and tough times, but knowing we are in His will trumps any difficulties we face. Hard to realize while we go through the rough waters, but true none the less.

It is frightening to set sail on the open waters of life and give our Father complete control, yet it is also the one thing in my life that has given me the most freedom. The freedom to be who God designed me to be – in His image, not my image or someone else. I no longer have to worry about who I am or what I am meant to be as I did in the past. My identity is in Christ alone and the roles I play are revealed as I listen to His promptings. No, I don't always get it right, but that's a part of the beauty of His guidance. If I am fully submitted to following Him, He is better able to use gentle nudges for path corrections. Too many times I have ignored communication with Him through prayer and scripture primarily, and have strayed too far off course. That is my stubborn nature and He has had to use what I call the spiritual 2x4 across my head to get my attention. While that's effective, nudges feel much better.

We are to continue growing and maturing in all areas of life; however, the decision to embrace the life of a devoted disciple never wavers. We need to try not to dwell on the past, but rather take brief glimpses back to discern what lessons we need to take away from mistakes. Knowing that our heavenly Father loves and accepts us unconditionally gives us the freedom to pursue His journey in the way He desires for us.

To be a disciple of Christ is to be someone who is focused, someone who is eager to learn. Someone eager to learn from the lives of those who were in the Bible, someone who is eager to learn from those around them, and eager to seek and actively respond to the promptings of the Holy Spirit. We are told to move off the milk and onto solid food as we go along this Christian journey. And as a disciple, that means we don't do things casually. We're not just casual Christians along for the ride. We cannot simply attend church, listen to something online, or watch TV sermons. That's not what a true disciple is.

A true disciple is active. A true disciple is trying to reflect and change their actions personally as they move forward to be more and more Christ-like. They are intentionally working on their attitudes and looking forward to what God has in store for them. They are engaged in conversations with people and living an active life for Christ. So what does it mean to mature? What is Christian maturity? What does that look like for a disciple? I've asked myself that many times over the years, especially early on as a Christian.

At first I thought it meant that the journey is a set of stairs. Possibly a ladder that I need to climb to become mature. It was something that could be measured by myself and others to show that I am more mature than my fellow believer in comparison. The Holy Spirit quickly showed me that I was way off-base and wrong. That's not what it is, not at all. The discipleship journey is not one that needs to be compared to others. Another thought was to simply follow what someone else has done, copying their movements and mimicking their path. That doesn't work either because the Holy Spirit has a unique path, a distinct journey for only you. As I've already said, sailing the open waters of life is not something that can be predicted. It's not something that can be expected. It must be actively lived out by experiencing.

This is the mindset you need to have to effectively go through this guide and follow the Holy Spirit as He leads. The questions are meant to prompt deep insight for you as an individual.

Some days

- will be more involved than others and take more time
- will be tougher than others as the Holy Spirit leads
- conversations will be raw and hurt to have with fellow believers
- you will experience breakthrough in unanticipated ways
- emotions will seem to be out of control

Every day is a day to be treasured as a disciple of Christ, no matter what our experiences may be. The hard work required to get through this stage of life and your marriage is undeniable and cannot be ignored, but it is worth it. My prayer is that you will sail through the rough waters of life intentionally, with determination and in complete obedience to the Holy Spirit.

Overview of the Book of James

The Epistle of James is a practical book in the New Testament focused on living out one's faith through good deeds and righteous behavior. It reads less like a theological treatise and more like a collection of wisdom teachings or a sermon, emphasizing that genuine faith inevitably produces tangible results in a believer's life.

Author and Date:

Author: Traditionally attributed to James, the brother (or half-brother) of Jesus. This James became a prominent leader in the early Jerusalem church (Acts 15). His background gave him significant authority, particularly among Jewish Christians.

Date: Generally considered one of the earliest New Testament writings, possibly dated between AD 45-50. This early dating places it before the Jerusalem Council (c. AD 49) and potentially before many of Paul's letters. Its strongly Jewish character and lack of reference to later controversies (like Gentile inclusion discussed in Acts 15) support this view.

Audience and Historical Context:

Audience: Explicitly addressed to "the twelve tribes scattered among the nations" (James 1:1), referring to Jewish Christians living outside Palestine (the Diaspora).

Historical Nuances:

   Diaspora Life: These scattered believers faced various **trials** (James 1:2), likely including social ostracization, economic hardship, and possibly localized persecution for their faith in Jesus as the Messiah.

   Socio-Economic Tensions: The letter strongly addresses issues of wealth and poverty (James 1:9-11, 2:1-7, 5:1-6). It condemns favoritism towards the rich within the church community and warns wealthy oppressors. This reflects the significant socio-economic disparities present in the Roman Empire and within early Christian communities.

   Jewish Roots: The letter is deeply immersed in **Jewish tradition and wisdom literature (like Proverbs). It frequently alludes to the Old Testament Law and prophets and uses Jewish figures like Abraham and Rahab as examples (James 2:21-25). It resonates strongly with the ethical teachings of Jesus, particularly the Sermon on the Mount.

   Early Church Practice: It provides insight into the practical challenges facing fledgling Christian communities: internal disputes (James 4:1-3), controlling speech (James 3:1-12), the need for practical care for the needy (James 2:15-16), and the importance of prayer (James 5:13-18).

Key Themes:

1. Perseverance Through Trials: Testing produces endurance and spiritual maturity.

2. Faith and Works: True, living faith is demonstrated by corresponding actions (not saved by works, but faith results in works).

3. Taming the Tongue: The immense power (for good or evil) of words.

4. Wisdom: Contrasting worldly wisdom with godly wisdom "from above."

5. Warning Against Partiality/Favoritism: Especially regarding the rich and poor.

6. Prayer: Emphasizing its power and importance in the believer's life.

In essence, James provides practical instructions for Christians facing real-world difficulties, urging them to live consistently with their professed faith, demonstrating its reality through tangible actions, ethical behavior, and reliance on God.

A fantastic resource for Bible overviews is The Bible Project at bibleproject.com/guides/book-of-james/. They include video overviews and graphic overviews like below.

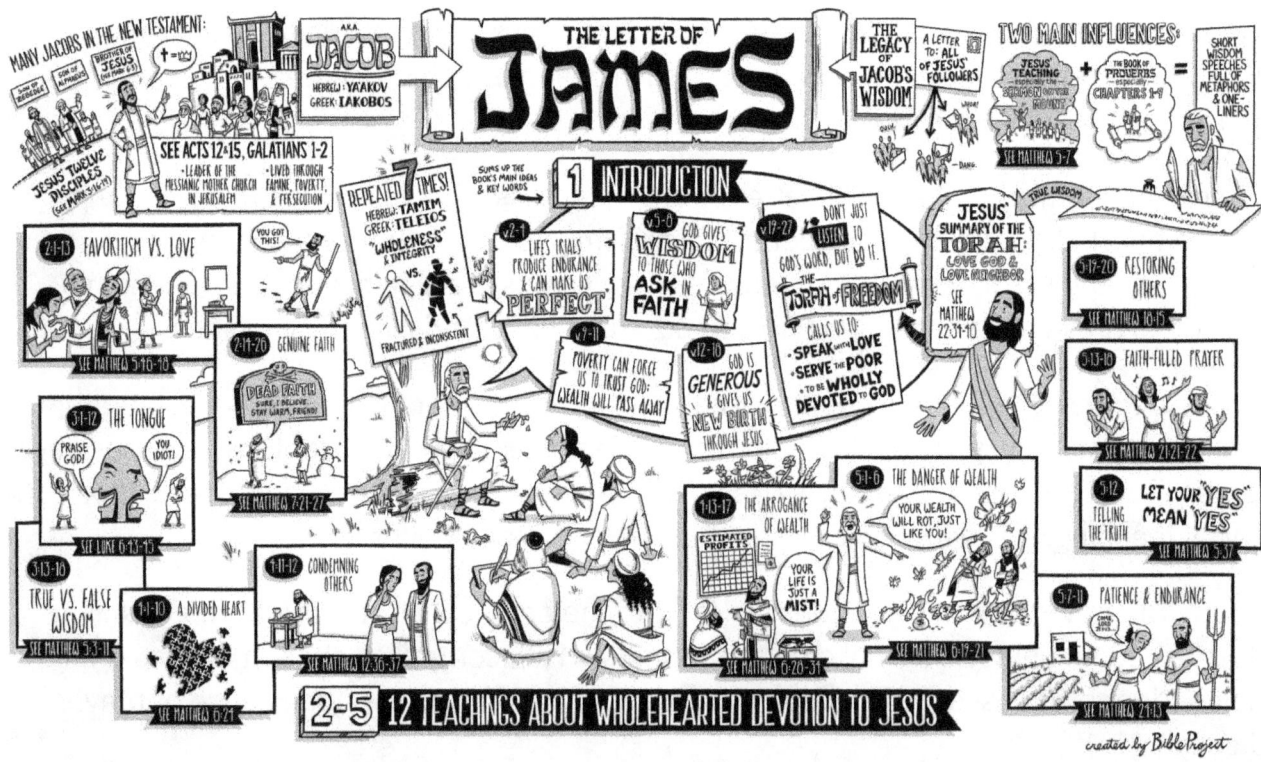

Day 1: Faith's Response to Trials

Scripture Passage (James 1:1-4, ESV)

1 James, a servant of God and of the Lord Jesus Christ, To the twelve tribes in the Dispersion: Greetings. 2 Count it all joy, my brothers, when you meet trials of various kinds, 3 for you know that the testing of your faith produces steadfastness. 4 And let steadfastness have its full effect, that you may be perfect and complete, lacking in nothing.

Points to Ponder:

1. How does the command to "Count it all joy" in trials challenge your typical emotional or behavioral response to difficulties? What does this *action* of counting show about underlying faith?

2. James states, "you know that the testing of your faith produces steadfastness." How does this knowledge fuel the *action* of joyful endurance rather than passive resignation? Where might a lack of this knowledge hinder a faith-filled response?

3. Steadfastness leads to being "perfect and complete, lacking in nothing." How does actively persevering through trials, as an act of faith, contribute to this spiritual maturity, rather than just passively waiting for trials to end?

Application Question:
Identify one trial, big or small, you are currently facing. What is one specific action you can take today to "count it joy," perhaps by thanking God for His presence or the opportunity for faith to be tested and grow?

Day 2: Seeking Wisdom Through Action

Scripture Passage (James 1:5-8, ESV)

5 If any of you lacks wisdom, let him ask God, who gives generously to all without reproach, and it will be given him. 6 But let him ask in faith, with no doubting, for the one who doubts is like a wave of the sea that is driven and tossed by the wind. 7 For that person must not suppose that he will receive anything from the Lord;8 he is a double-minded man, unstable in all his ways.

Points to Ponder:

1. Asking God for wisdom is presented as a necessary *action* when facing challenges (like the trials mentioned previously). How does viewing prayer for wisdom as an *act of faith* change your approach compared to seeing it as a last resort?

2. James stresses asking "in faith, with no doubting." How does doubt manifest itself not just as an internal feeling, but as something that affects the *action* of prayer and hinders receiving from God?

3. A "double-minded man" is described as "unstable in all his ways" (actions). How does a lack of unwavering faith (being double-minded) prevent consistent, decisive action in living out one's beliefs?

Application Question:
In what specific situation today do you lack wisdom? Take the action James prescribes: ask God specifically for wisdom regarding that situation, consciously choosing to trust His generous character rather than doubting.

Day 3: Faith's Perspective on Wealth and Poverty

Scripture Passage (James 1:9-11, ESV)

> 9 Let the lowly brother boast in his exaltation, 10 and the rich in his humiliation, because like a flower of the grass he will pass away. 11 For the sun rises with its scorching heat and withers the grass; its flower falls, and its beauty perishes. So also will the rich man fade away in the midst of his pursuits.

Points to Ponder:

1. Boasting is an *action* or attitude. How does faith in Christ enable the "lowly brother" to actively boast in his spiritual exaltation, rather than remaining defined by worldly circumstances?

2. For the rich, boasting "in his humiliation" is a counter-intuitive *action*. How does genuine faith lead to the active recognition of wealth's temporary nature and foster humility instead of pride?

3. How does the *action* of finding one's primary identity and worth in Christ, rather than in economic status, demonstrate a faith that values eternal realities over temporary ones?

Application Question:
Whether you consider yourself rich, poor, or somewhere in between, what is one concrete action you can take today to show that your ultimate worth and security come from Christ, not your financial situation (e.g., giving generously, thanking God for spiritual riches, avoiding status comparisons)?

Day 4: Steadfast Faith Receives the Crown

Scripture Passage (James 1:12, ESV)

> 12 Blessed is the man who remains steadfast under trial, for when he has stood the test he will receive the crown of life, which God has promised to those who love him.

Points to Ponder:

1. "Remains steadfast" implies active endurance, not passive waiting. What specific *actions* characterize someone who is remaining steadfast under trial, demonstrating their faith?

2. The promise of the "crown of life" is linked to having "stood the test." How does this future reward motivate present *action* (steadfastness) during difficult times?

3. The promise is specifically "to those who love him." How does love for God, born of faith, fuel the *action* of steadfast perseverance when trials tempt you to give up?

Application Question:
Think about a current or recent challenge that is testing your endurance. What is one specific action, motivated by faith and love for God, that you can take to "remain steadfast" today?

Day 5: Faith Recognizes the Source of Temptation

Scripture Passage (James 1:13-15, ESV)

13 Let no one say when he is tempted, "I am being tempted by God," for God cannot be tempted with evil, and he himself tempts no one. 14 But each person is tempted when he is lured and enticed by his own desire. 15 Then desire when it has conceived gives birth to sin, and sin when it is fully grown brings forth death.

Points to Ponder:

1. Blaming God during temptation is a forbidden *action* ("Let no one say..."). How does understanding God's character (He cannot tempt) based on faith prevent this wrong reaction and encourage personal responsibility?

2. James identifies "own desire" as the source of temptation. How does recognizing this internal source empower you to take proactive *action* against temptation, rather than feeling like a passive victim of external forces?

3. The progression is desire -> sin -> death. How does seeing sin not just as a forbidden act, but as the result of unchecked desire leading ultimately to death, motivate the *action* of resisting desire at its conception?

Application Question:
Identify one desire that frequently tempts you toward sin. What specific action can you take today, relying on God's strength, to interrupt the progression from desire to sin?

Day 6: Faith Recognizes the Source of Goodness

Scripture Passage (James 1:16-18, ESV)

16 Do not be deceived, my beloved brothers. 17 Every good gift and every perfect gift is from above, coming down from the Father of lights, with whom there is no variation or shadow due to change. 18 Of his own will he brought us forth by the word of truth, that we should be a kind of firstfruits of his creatures.

Points to Ponder:

1. How does the *action* of consciously recognizing God as the source of "every good gift" combat deception and cultivate gratitude and trust, rather than taking things for granted or attributing success solely to self?

2. God "brought us forth by the word of truth" – an act of His will. How does understanding our new birth as God's initiative motivate us to live differently, taking *actions* that reflect our status as His "firstfruits"?

3. God is unchanging ("no variation or shadow due to change"). How does faith in His stable, good character provide a firm foundation for consistent, faithful *action* in our own lives, even when circumstances change?

Application Question:
What is one specific "good gift" in your life right now? Take the action of explicitly thanking the "Father of lights" for it today, acknowledging Him as the source.

Day 7: Faith Listens Before Acting

Scripture Passage (James 1:19-21, ESV)

19 Know this, my beloved brothers: let every person be quick to hear, slow to speak, slow to anger; 20 for the anger of man does not produce the righteousness of God. 21 Therefore put away all filthiness and rampant wickedness and receive with meekness the implanted word, which is able to save your souls.

Points to Ponder:

1. Being "quick to hear, slow to speak, slow to anger" are specific commands for *action* in communication. How does practicing these actions demonstrate faith and trust in God's control, rather than reacting impulsively?

2. Human anger "does not produce the righteousness of God." How does this truth motivate the difficult *action* of controlling anger, recognizing it as an ineffective tool for achieving godly outcomes?

3. "Put away all filthiness" and "receive with meekness the implanted word" are necessary *actions* for spiritual growth. How does active repentance and humble reception prepare your heart to not just hear the Word, but to allow it to take root and produce righteous *actions*?

Application Question:
In your conversations today, consciously practice the action of being "quick to hear." Focus on truly listening to understand before formulating your response.

Day 8: Faith is Doing, Not Just Hearing

Scripture Passage (James 1:22-25, ESV)

22 But be doers of the word, and not hearers only, deceiving yourselves. 23 For if anyone is a hearer of the word and not a doer, he is like a man who looks intently at his natural face in a mirror. 24 For he looks at himself and goes away and at once forgets what he was like. 25 But the one who looks into the perfect law, the law of liberty, and perseveres, being no hearer who forgets but a doer who acts, he will be blessed in his doing.

Points to Ponder:

1. James warns that being "hearers only" leads to self-deception. In what areas might you be hearing God's Word without translating it into *action*, potentially deceiving yourself about your spiritual condition?

2. Contrast the *action* of the man who glances in the mirror and forgets with the one who "looks intently into the perfect law... and perseveres." What kind of active engagement with God's Word does this imply is necessary for it to lead to action?

3. Blessing is promised to the "doer who acts" and comes "in his doing." How does this link between obedience (action) and blessing challenge the idea that faith is purely internal or passive?

Application Question:
Recall one specific truth or command from Scripture you have heard recently. What is one concrete action, however small, you can take today to be a "doer" of that word?

Day 9: Faith Acts Religiously

Scripture Passage (James 1:26-27, ESV)

26 If anyone thinks he is religious and does not bridle his tongue but deceives his heart, this person's religion is worthless. 27 Religion that is pure and undefiled before God the Father is this: to visit orphans and widows in their affliction, and to keep oneself unstained from the world.

Points to Ponder:

1. James defines "worthless" religion by a lack of *action* – specifically, failing to "bridle his tongue." How does uncontrolled speech betray a disconnect between professed faith and actual practice?

2. "Pure and undefiled religion" involves specific *actions*: compassionate care ("visit orphans and widows") and personal holiness ("keep oneself unstained"). Why are these outward actions presented as essential indicators of genuine faith, rather than optional extras?

3. How does the *action* of visiting those in affliction show the heart of God and the reality of one's faith in a way that mere religious sentiment cannot?

Application Question:
Consider the three marks of true religion here (controlled speech, care for the vulnerable, personal purity). Choose one area and identify a specific action you can take this week to demonstrate "pure and undefiled religion."

Day 10: Faith Rejects Partiality

Scripture Passage (James 2:1-4, ESV)

1 My brothers, show no partiality as you hold the faith in our Lord Jesus Christ, the Lord of glory. 2 For if a man wearing a gold ring and fine clothing comes into your assembly, and a poor man in shabby clothing also comes in, 3 and if you pay attention to the one who wears the fine clothing and say, "You sit here in a good place," while you say to the poor man, "You stand over there," or, "Sit down at my feet," 4 have you not then made distinctions among yourselves and become judges with evil thoughts?

Points to Ponder:

1. James directly links holding faith in Jesus with the *action* of showing no partiality. Why is the act of treating people differently based on wealth or status incompatible with faith in the "Lord of glory"?

2. The scenario describes specific *actions*: giving preferential treatment to the rich and dismissive treatment to the poor. How do these actions reveal underlying "evil thoughts" and judgments that contradict faith?

3. In what subtle ways might you make distinctions or judgments based on external appearances or social standing? How can faith motivate the *action* of treating all individuals with equal dignity as image-bearers of God?

Application Question:
Be intentionally observant today of how you interact with people from different socioeconomic backgrounds (in person, online, or even in your thoughts). What one action can you take to actively counter any tendency towards partiality?

Day 11: Faith Aligns with God's Choice

Scripture Passage (James 2:5-7, ESV)

> 5 Listen, my beloved brothers, has not God chosen those who are poor in the world to be rich in faith and heirs of the kingdom, which he has promised to those who love him? 6 But you have dishonored the poor man. Are not the rich the ones who oppress you, and the ones who drag you into court? 7 Are they not the ones who blaspheme the honorable name by which you were called?

Points to Ponder:

1. God has "chosen those who are poor... to be rich in faith." How should this truth about God's perspective influence the *actions* and attitudes of believers towards those less fortunate?

2. James accuses his readers of the *action* of dishonoring the poor, directly contradicting God's choice. How does this reveal a faith that is more aligned with worldly values than with God's heart?

3. The rich who were being favored were often the ones acting unjustly ("oppress you," "drag you into court," "blaspheme"). How does recognizing this irony expose the foolishness of acting partially based on worldly status rather than godly principle?

Application Question:
How can you take action this week to specifically honor or affirm the faith and dignity of someone who might be considered "poor in the world" but is "rich in faith"?

Day 12: Faith Fulfills the Royal Law

Scripture Passage (James 2:8-11, ESV)

8 If you really fulfill the royal law according to the Scripture, "You shall love your neighbor as yourself," you are doing well. 9 But if you show partiality, you are committing sin and are convicted by the law as transgressors. 10 For whoever keeps the whole law but fails in one point has become guilty of all of it. 11 For he who said, "Do not commit adultery," also said, "Do not murder." If you do not commit adultery but do murder, you have become a transgressor of the law.

Points to Ponder:

1. Loving your neighbor as yourself is called the "royal law." How is this commandment about *action* rather than just sentiment?

2. Showing partiality is explicitly called "committing sin" and makes one a "transgressor" of this royal law. How does this elevate the *action* of impartiality from mere politeness to a matter of obedience to God's core command?

3. James argues that failing in one point of the law makes one guilty of all. How does this principle underscore the importance of consistency in our faith-driven *actions*, showing that we cannot pick and choose which parts of God's law to obey?

Application Question:
Think of "love your neighbor as yourself" as a call to action. What is one specific, practical way you can actively love a neighbor (literal or figurative) today, ensuring your action is impartial?

Day 13: Faith Acts Mercifully

Scripture Passage (James 2:12-13, ESV)

12 So speak and so act as those who are to be judged under the law of liberty. 13 For judgment is without mercy to one who has shown no mercy. Mercy triumphs over judgment.

Points to Ponder:

1. We are called to "speak and so act" in light of future judgment under the "law of liberty." How does understanding that our words and deeds will be judged motivate us to ensure our *actions* align with our faith?

2. "Judgment is without mercy to one who has shown no mercy." How does this principle highlight the critical importance of the *action* of showing mercy as evidence of received mercy?

3. "Mercy triumphs over judgment." How does faith in God's triumphant mercy empower and motivate us to actively extend mercy to others in our words and *actions*?

Application Question:
Identify a situation or relationship where you have an opportunity to show mercy today. What specific action can you take to extend mercy, reflecting the mercy you have received from God?

Day 14: Faith Without Action is Dead

Scripture Passage (James 2:14-17, ESV)

14 What good is it, my brothers, if someone says he has faith but does not have works? Can that faith save him? 15 If a brother or sister is poorly clothed and lacking in daily food, 16 and one of you says to them, "Go in peace, be warmed and filled," without giving them the things needed for the body, what good is that? 17 So also faith by itself, if it does not have works, is dead.

Points to Ponder:

1. James asks, "What good is it... Can that faith save him?" regarding faith without works. How does this challenge the notion that belief can be entirely separated from practical *action* and still be considered saving faith?

2. The example given contrasts empty words with tangible *action* ("giving them the things needed for the body"). When have your *actions* (or lack thereof) failed to match your words of concern or blessing?

3. "Faith by itself, if it does not have works, is dead." What does this metaphor of "dead" faith suggest about the nature of a belief system that produces no outward *action* or fruit?

Application Question:
Is there someone you know with a tangible need ("poorly clothed," "lacking in daily food," or a modern equivalent)? Instead of just offering words, what specific action can you take to help meet that need, demonstrating living faith?

Day 15: Faith is Shown by Action

Scripture Passage (James 2:18-20, ESV)

18 But someone will say, "You have faith and I have works." Show me your faith apart from your works, and I will show you my faith by my works. 19 You believe that God is one; you do well. Even the demons believe—and shudder! 20 Do you want to be shown, you foolish person, that faith apart from works is useless?

Points to Ponder:

1. James's challenge is "Show me your faith... I will show you my faith *by* my works." How does this statement establish *actions* (works) as the visible evidence or proof of invisible faith?

2. Even demons possess intellectual belief ("believe that God is one") but lack saving faith. How does this stark comparison highlight that genuine faith must involve more than mental assent and must result in transformative *action*?

3. Faith apart from works is called "useless." In what ways is a faith that produces no tangible *action* or change ineffective or pointless in the believer's life and in its impact on the world?

Application Question:
Think about a specific aspect of your Christian faith (e.g., belief in God's love, forgiveness, call to serve). What is one action you can intentionally take this week that clearly demonstrates that belief to others?

Day 16: Faith Proven by Action: Abraham

Scripture Passage (James 2:21-24, ESV)

21 Was not Abraham our father justified by works when he offered up his son Isaac on the altar? 22 You see that faith was active along with his works, and faith was completed by his works; 23 and the Scripture was fulfilled that says, "Abraham believed God, and it was counted to him as righteousness" — and he was called a friend of God. 24 You see that a person is justified by works and not by faith alone.

Points to Ponder:

1. Abraham's faith was declared long before Genesis 22, yet James says he was "justified by works when he offered up his son Isaac." How does this specific, costly *action show* the reality and depth of his pre-existing faith?

2. "Faith was active along with his works, and faith was completed by his works." How does this description show faith and *action* working together, with the action bringing the faith to its intended fulfillment or proof?

3. James concludes, "a person is justified by works and not by faith alone." How does Abraham's example illustrate that the kind of faith that justifies is never "alone" but always expresses itself through obedient *action*?

Application Question:
What is a situation currently demanding costly obedience or action from you? How can Abraham's example encourage you to act in faith, trusting that your action demonstrates and "completes" your faith?

Day 17: Faith Proven by Action: Rahab

Scripture Passage (James 2:25-26, ESV)

25 And in the same way was not also Rahab the prostitute justified by works when she received the messengers and sent them out by another way? 26 For as the body apart from the spirit is dead, so also faith apart from works is dead.

Points to Ponder:

1. Rahab, a Gentile and a prostitute, is also presented as justified by her *actions*. What does her example show about the universality of the principle that faith demonstrates itself through works, regardless of background?

2. What specific *actions* did Rahab take that showed her faith in the God of Israel, even at great personal risk?

3. The final analogy: "faith apart from works is dead" like a body without a spirit. How does this powerful image summarize James's entire argument in this chapter about the necessity of *an action* as evidence of living faith?

Application Question:
Rahab acted decisively based on what she believed about God. What is one decisive action you can take this week based on your faith, perhaps involving stepping out of your comfort zone or taking a risk for God?

Day 18: Faith Controls the Tongue (Part 1)

Scripture Passage (James 3:1-4, ESV)

1 Not many of you should become teachers, my brothers, for you know that we who teach will be judged with greater strictness. 2 For we all stumble in many ways. And if anyone does not stumble in what he says, he is a perfect man, able also to bridle his whole body. 3 If we put bits into the mouths of horses so that they obey us, we guide their whole bodies as well. 4 Look at the ships also: though they are so large and are driven by strong winds, they are guided by a very small rudder wherever the will of the pilot directs.

Points to Ponder:

1. Teaching involves the *action* of speaking. Why does James connect this action with "greater strictness" in judgment, highlighting the responsibility that comes with influential speech?

2. Controlling speech ("not stumble in what he says") is presented as a mark of maturity ("a perfect man") and the key to controlling all other *actions* ("bridle his whole body"). Why is this specific action of speech control so indicative of overall spiritual discipline?

3. The analogies of the bit and the rudder show small things directing large things. How do these images illustrate the power of our words (an *action*) to direct the course of our lives and influence others?

Application Question:
Consider the influence your words have. What is one specific action you can take today to use your speech to guide yourself or others in a positive, godly direction?

Day 19: Faith Controls the Tongue (Part 2)

Scripture Passage (James 3:5-8, ESV)

5 So also the tongue is a small member, yet it boasts of great things. How great a forest is set ablaze by such a small fire! 6 And the tongue is a fire, a world of unrighteousness. The tongue is set among our members, staining the whole body, setting on fire the entire course of life, and set on fire by hell. 7 For every kind of beast and bird, of reptile and sea creature, can be tamed and has been tamed by mankind, 8 but no human being can tame the tongue. It is a restless evil, full of deadly poison.

Points to Ponder:

1. The tongue's *action* is compared to a fire that can cause widespread destruction. Reflect on times when words (yours or others') have had a disproportionately large negative impact. How does this reinforce the need for faith-based control?

2. The tongue is called "a world of unrighteousness... staining the whole body... set on fire by hell." How does this powerful language reveal the serious spiritual dimension behind the *action* of uncontrolled, ungodly speech?

3. "No human being can tame the tongue." How does acknowledging this limitation drive you to the *action* of depending on God's power and grace to control your speech, rather than relying solely on willpower?

<u>Application Question:</u>
Since human effort alone cannot tame the tongue, what specific action of faith can you take today? Perhaps pray specifically for God's help before entering a potentially difficult conversation or commit to pausing before speaking reactively.

Day 20: Faith Produces Consistent Speech

Scripture Passage (James 3:9-12, ESV)

9 With it we bless our Lord and Father, and with it we curse people who are made in the likeness of God. 10 From the same mouth come blessing and cursing. My brothers, these things ought not to be so. 11 Does a spring pour forth from the same opening both fresh and salt water? 12 Can a fig tree, my brothers, bear olives, or a grapevine produce figs? Neither can a salt pond yield fresh water.

Points to Ponder:

1. James highlights the contradictory *action* of blessing God and cursing people made in His image. How does this inconsistency in speech reveal an inconsistency in the heart or faith from which it flows?

2. "These things ought not to be so." How does this simple statement challenge you to pursue integrity and consistency in the *action* of speaking, ensuring your words align with your professed faith?

3. The nature analogies (spring, fig tree) emphasize that a source produces according to its nature. How does this illustrate that genuine faith should naturally produce consistently good *actions*, including speech, flowing from a transformed heart?

Application Question:
Pay attention to your speech patterns today. Is there an inconsistency (e.g., praising God in church, gossiping at work)? What one action can you take to bring your speech into greater alignment with your faith?

Day 21: Faith Shows Wisdom Through Action

Scripture Passage (James 3:13-16, ESV)

13 Who is wise and understanding among you? By his good conduct let him show his works in the meekness of wisdom. 14 But if you have bitter jealousy and selfish ambition in your hearts, do not boast and be false to the truth. 15 This is not the wisdom that comes down from above, but is earthly, unspiritual, demonic. 16 For where jealousy and selfish ambition exist, there will be disorder and every vile practice.

Points to Ponder:

1. True wisdom is not merely knowledge but is demonstrated ("show") by specific *actions* ("good conduct," "works") performed with a specific attitude ("meekness"). How does this definition challenge purely intellectual or theoretical approaches to faith and wisdom?

2. Bitter jealousy and selfish ambition are internal states, but they lead to negative *actions* ("boast," "be false," "disorder," "vile practice"). How do your internal motives shape your external actions, revealing the type of "wisdom" you are operating under?

3. The source of wisdom determines the resulting actions (heavenly wisdom leads to good conduct; earthly/demonic wisdom leads to disorder). How can you actively cultivate heavenly wisdom through faith so that your *actions* reflect God's character?

Application Question:
Consider a situation where you might be tempted by selfish ambition or jealousy today. What specific action, characterized by "meekness of wisdom," can you choose instead?

Day 22: Faith Pursues Heavenly Wisdom's Actions

Scripture Passage (James 3:17-18, ESV)

17 But the wisdom from above is first pure, then peaceable, gentle, open to reason, full of mercy and good fruits, impartial and sincere. 18 And a harvest of righteousness is sown in peace by those who make peace.

Points to Ponder:

1. Verse 17 lists the characteristics of heavenly wisdom, which are expressed through *actions* and attitudes (peaceable, gentle, merciful, etc.). Which of these qualities do you most need faith to help you actively cultivate in your conduct?

2. This wisdom is "full of mercy and good fruits." What kinds of specific *actions* ("good fruits") would you expect to see flowing from a life guided by this wisdom?

3. Peacemaking is presented as an *action* ("those who make peace") that actively sows seeds, resulting in a "harvest of righteousness." How does actively pursuing peace in relationships demonstrate faith and contribute to godly outcomes?

Application Question:
Choose one characteristic of heavenly wisdom (pure, peaceable, gentle, open to reason, merciful, impartial, sincere). What is one specific action you can take today to intentionally practice that quality in an interaction?

Day 23: Faith Battles Worldly Actions

Scripture Passage (James 4:1-3, ESV)

1 What causes quarrels and what causes fights among you? Is it not this, that your passions are at war within you? 2 You desire and do not have, so you murder. You covet and cannot obtain, so you fight and quarrel. You do not have, because you do not ask. 3 You ask and do not receive, because you ask wrongly, to spend it on your passions.

Points to Ponder:

1. James traces outward *actions* like quarrels and fights back to internal "passions at war within." How does understanding this connection help you address conflict not just by modifying behavior, but by dealing with the underlying desires through faith?

2. Unmet desire leads to destructive *actions* (murder/hatred, coveting, fighting). How does faith offer a different way to handle unmet desires, preventing them from erupting into sinful actions?

3. Even the seemingly good *action* of prayer ("ask") is ineffective if the motive is wrong ("ask wrongly, to spend it on your passions"). How does this show that faith must purify not only our outward actions but also the intentions behind them?

Application Question:
When you feel conflict or frustration rising today, pause and take the action of identifying the underlying "passion" or desire. Pray about that desire, asking God to purify your motives rather than letting it lead to sinful action.

Day 24: Faith Chooses God Over the World

Scripture Passage (James 4:4-6, ESV)

4 You adulterous people! Do you not know that friendship with the world is enmity with God? Therefore whoever wishes to be a friend of the world makes himself an enemy of God. 5 Or do you suppose it is to no purpose that the Scripture says, "He yearns jealously over the spirit that he has made to dwell in us"? 6 But he gives more grace. Therefore it says, "God opposes the proud but gives grace to the humble."

Points to Ponder:

1. "Friendship with the world" involves embracing its values and ways, often demonstrated through *actions*. Why is this active choice presented so starkly as making oneself God's enemy?

2. God "yearns jealously" for our undivided allegiance. How does recognizing God's passionate love motivate the *action* of choosing Him wholeheartedly over worldly attractions?

3. God gives grace to the humble but opposes the proud. How is humility, expressed through *actions* of dependence and submission, the key to accessing the grace needed to resist worldliness and live faithfully?

Application Question:
Identify one specific area where the "world's" values conflict with God's values (e.g., materialism, status-seeking, self-reliance). What action can you take today to demonstrate your allegiance to God in that area, humbly relying on His grace?

Day 25: Faith Acts in Submission and Resistance

Scripture Passage (James 4:7-10, ESV)

7 Submit yourselves therefore to God. Resist the devil, and he will flee from you. 8 Draw near to God, and he will draw near to you. Cleanse your hands, you sinners, and purify your hearts, you double-minded. 9 Be wretched and mourn and weep. Let your laughter be turned to mourning and your joy to gloom. 10 Humble yourselves before the Lord, and he will exalt you.

Points to Ponder:

1. This passage contains a series of commands requiring decisive *action*: Submit, Resist, Draw near, Cleanse, Purify, Mourn, Humble yourselves. Why is such active engagement necessary for overcoming sin and worldliness, rather than passive belief?

2. "Cleanse your hands" refers to outward *actions*, while "purify your hearts" refers to inner motives. Why does James insist on both internal and external transformation as necessary actions of faith?

3. Each *action* we take (Submit, Resist, Draw Near, Humble) is met with a corresponding divine response (Devil flees, God draws near, God exalts). How does this promise encourage bold, faith-filled action?

Application Question:
Choose one of the active commands from this passage (Submit, Resist, Draw Near, Cleanse/Purify, Mourn/Repent, Humble). Focus on putting that specific action into practice throughout your day today.

Day 26: Faith Refuses Judgmental Speech

Scripture Passage (James 4:11-12, ESV)

11 Do not speak evil against one another, brothers. The one who speaks against a brother or judges his brother, speaks evil against the law and judges the law. But if you judge the law, you are not a doer of the law but a judge. 12 There is only one lawgiver and judge, he who is able to save and to destroy. But who are you to judge your neighbor?

Points to Ponder:

1. Speaking evil and judging are forbidden *actions*. How does engaging in such speech show a lack of faith in God's role as the rightful Judge and Lawgiver?

2. James argues that judging a brother is equivalent to judging the law itself. How does this perspective shift the focus from the perceived faults of others to the inappropriate *action* of the one judging?

3. Instead of judging the law (or others by it), we are called to be "doers of the law." How does faith express itself through the positive *action* of obedience and love, rather than the negative action of criticism and judgment?

Application Question:
When tempted to speak negatively or judgmentally about someone today, consciously take the action of stopping yourself. Instead, either pray for that person or find something positive to say (or remain silent).

Day 27: Faith Plans with God

Scripture Passage (James 4:13-17, ESV)

13 Come now, you who say, "Today or tomorrow we will go into such and such a town and spend a year there and trade and make a profit"— 14 yet you do not know what tomorrow will bring. What is your life? For you are a mist that appears for a little time and then vanishes. 15 Instead you ought to say, "If the Lord wills, we will live and do this or that." 16 As it is, you boast in your arrogance. All such boasting is evil. 17 So whoever knows the right thing to do and fails to do it, for him it is sin.

Points to Ponder:

1. The *action* condemned here is arrogant planning that ignores God. How does acknowledging life's brevity ("you are a mist") and God's sovereignty motivate the different *action* of planning with dependence ("If the Lord wills")?

2. Saying "If the Lord wills" is more than just words; it's an *action* reflecting a heart attitude of submission. How can you incorporate this faith-filled posture into your daily planning and decision-making actions?

3. Verse 17 provides a crucial definition of sin: knowing the right *action* ("the right thing to do") and failing to perform it. How does this principle summarize the core message of James about the necessity of acting on one's faith?

Application Question:
As you think about your plans for tomorrow or this week, consciously practice the action of submitting them to God. Perhaps write "DV" (Deo Volente - God willing) next to them or simply pray, "Lord, if you will, help me to do this."

Day 28: Faith, Wealth, and Justice

Scripture Passage (James 5:1-6, ESV)

1 Come now, you rich, weep and howl for the miseries that are coming upon you. 2 Your riches have rotted and your garments are moth-eaten. 3 Your gold and silver have corroded, and their corrosion will be evidence against you and will eat your flesh like fire. You have laid up treasure in the last days. 4 Behold, the wages of the laborers who mowed your fields, which you kept back by fraud, are crying out against you, and the cries of the harvesters have reached the ears of the Lord of hosts. 5 You have lived on the earth in luxury and in self-indulgence. You have fattened your hearts in a day of slaughter. 6 You have condemned and murdered the righteous person. He does not resist you.

Points to Ponder:

1. This passage condemns specific *actions* of the unjust rich: hoarding wealth, fraud, luxury at others' expense, oppression. How does this serve as a negative example, highlighting the kinds of actions that are diametrically opposed to genuine faith?

2. The withheld wages "are crying out." How does this personification show that unjust *actions*, particularly economic exploitation, have spiritual consequences and are seen by God?

3. While addressed to the "rich," what warnings does this passage contain for all believers regarding the *actions* associated with handling money and dealing with others in financial or employment contexts? How should faith lead to actions of justice and fairness?

Application Question:
Examine your own financial actions and attitudes. Are there any areas where you could act more justly, fairly, or generously, reflecting the values of God's kingdom rather than the practices condemned here? Take one step in that direction this week.

Day 29: Faith Acts Patiently and Honestly

Scripture Passage (James 5:7-12, ESV)

> 7 Be patient, therefore, brothers, until the coming of the Lord. See how the farmer waits for the precious fruit of the earth, being patient about it, until it receives the early and the late rains. 8 You also, be patient. Establish your hearts, for the coming of the Lord is at hand. 9 Do not grumble against one another, brothers, so that you may not be judged; behold, the Judge is standing at the door. 10 As an example of suffering and patience, brothers, take the prophets who spoke in the name of the Lord. 11 Behold, we consider those blessed who remained steadfast. You have heard of the steadfastness of Job, and you have seen the purpose of the Lord, how the Lord is compassionate and merciful. 12 But above all, my brothers, do not swear, either by heaven or by earth or by any other oath, but let your "yes" be yes and your "no" be no, so that you may not fall under condemnation.

Points to Ponder:

1. Patience is presented as an *action* ("Be patient," "Establish your hearts") motivated by the Lord's coming. How does faith in Christ's return empower the active endurance needed to wait patiently without giving up?

2. Avoiding grumbling and speaking truthfully ("let your 'yes' be yes...") are specific *actions* commanded. How do these actions demonstrate a faith that trusts God's timing and values integrity?

3. The examples of the farmer, prophets, and Job illustrate steadfastness through difficult circumstances. How does reflecting on their faith-filled *actions* encourage your own perseverance?

Application Question:
In what situation today do you need to practice the action of patience? Alternatively, focus on the action of integrity: ensure your "yes" truly means yes and your "no" means no in all your commitments and conversations.

Day 30: Faith Acts Through Prayer and Restoration

Scripture Passage (James 5:13-20, ESV)

13 Is anyone among you suffering? Let him pray. Is anyone cheerful? Let him sing praise. 14 Is anyone among you sick? Let him call for the elders of the church, and let them pray over him, anointing him with oil in the name of the Lord. 15 And the prayer of faith will save the one who is sick, and the Lord will raise him up. And if he has committed sins, he will be forgiven. 16 Therefore, confess your sins to one another and pray for one another, that you may be healed. The prayer of a righteous person has great power as it is working. 17 Elijah was a man with a nature like ours, and he prayed fervently that it might not rain, and for three years and six months it did not rain on the earth. 18 Then he prayed again, and heaven gave rain, and the earth bore its fruit. 19 My brothers, if anyone among you wanders from the truth and someone brings him back, 20 let him know that whoever brings back a sinner from his wandering will save his soul from death and will cover a multitude of sins.

Points to Ponder:

1. Prayer, praise, calling elders, confession, and praying for one another are all presented as specific *actions* prompted by different life circumstances. How does viewing prayer as an active response of faith, rather than a passive wish, change your approach to it?

2. The "prayer of faith" is described as having powerful effects (saving, raising up, forgiving, healing). How does this emphasis on the power inherent in the *action* of faith-filled prayer motivate you to pray more expectantly and persistently?

3. Bringing back a wandering believer is a significant *action* with eternal consequences ("save his soul from death"). How does this final instruction encapsulate the practical, restorative nature of the active faith James has described throughout the letter?

Application Question:
Choose one action from this passage: Pray for someone suffering, sing praise, ask for prayer if sick, confess a sin to a trusted believer, pray for someone else's healing, or take a step to gently restore someone wandering from the truth. Put that action into practice this week.

Day 31: Living Out James - Faith That Acts

Purpose: Today is for reflecting on the entire journey through James and synthesizing its core message about the inseparable nature of faith and action. Consider the following questions prayerfully, reviewing notes from previous days if helpful.

Summation Questions:

1. Looking back over the past 30 days, what are the 2-3 most significant ways James has challenged your understanding or practice of faith? How did examining specific *actions* (or lack thereof) in areas like trials, speech, partiality, or prayer reveal the state of your faith?

2. James consistently contrasts "hearing only" (1:22) with "doing," "dead faith" (2:17, 26) with living faith demonstrated by Abraham and Rahab [10], and worldly wisdom with heavenly wisdom shown by works (3:13-18).[29] How does this pattern reinforce the central theme that real faith must actively express itself?

3. James emphasizes specific *actions*: controlling the tongue (Ch 3) [8], showing impartiality and caring for the poor (Ch 2) [7], patience in suffering (Ch 1 & 5) [6], humble submission to God (Ch 4) [5], and prayer (Ch 5).[9] Which of these action areas represents the biggest growth opportunity for you right now, and why?

4. How does James's teaching on faith and works (esp. 2:14-26) relate to other New Testament teachings on salvation by grace through faith (e.g., Ephesians 2:8-10)? How can both perspectives be true and complementary? (Consider works as the necessary *evidence* or *fruit* of genuine saving faith, rather than the *means* of earning salvation).

5. James concludes by highlighting the *action* of restoring a wandering believer (5:19-20).[38] How does this final charge encapsulate the practical, active, and restorative nature of the faith James describes? What specific step can you take this month to live out this kind of restorative faith in your community?

Table: James's Marks of Living Faith: From Belief to Action

Passage/Theme	Required Action/Demonstration of Faith
James 1:2-4 Trials	Count trials joy, actively persevere to develop steadfastness
James 1:5-8 Wisdom	Ask God for wisdom in faith, without doubting
James 1:9-11 Status	Find worth in spiritual reality, not temporary wealth/poverty
James 1:19-21 Hearing	Be quick to hear, slow to speak/anger; put away sin, receive Word humbly
James 1:22-25 Hearing/Doing	Be doers of the Word, not just hearers; act on the law of liberty
James 1:26-27 Religion	Bridle tongue, visit orphans/widows, keep unstained from the world
James 2:1-13 Partiality	Show no partiality, actively love neighbor as self, act mercifully
James 2:14-26 Faith/Works	Meet practical needs; demonstrate faith by works; works complete faith
James 3:1-12 Tongue	Control speech; recognize its power; seek consistency (blessing, not cursing)
James 3:13-18 Wisdom	Show heavenly wisdom by good conduct, meekness, peace, mercy, good fruits
James 4:1-10 Worldliness/Humility	Resist passions/world; submit to God, resist devil, draw near, cleanse, humble self
James 4:11-12 Judging	Do not speak evil or judge others; leave judgment to God
James 4:13-17 Planning	Acknowledge God's will in plans ("If the Lord wills"); do the known good
James 5:1-6 Wealth	Act justly with resources; avoid exploitation and self-indulgence

James 5:7-12 Patience/Honesty	Be patient awaiting Lord's return; don't grumble; let "Yes" be yes
James 5:13-20 Prayer/Restoration	Pray in faith in all circumstances; confess; pray for others; restore wanderers

Conclusion: The Ongoing Journey of Active Faith

The journey through the Book of James powerfully underscores a vital truth: genuine faith is dynamic and demonstrative. James does not present a dichotomy between faith and works, but rather an integrated reality where authentic belief inevitably overflows into tangible action. Throughout the epistle, from enduring trials with joy to controlling the tongue, showing impartiality, and praying expectantly, James calls believers to live out their professed faith in the concrete realities of daily life.

The consistent message is that actions serve as the evidence, the fruit, and the completion of a living faith. A faith that produces no change in behavior, no compassionate response to need, no effort towards holiness and justice, is questioned as being merely intellectual assent, like that of demons, or described as "dead" and "useless". Conversely, actions rooted in heavenly wisdom, motivated by love for God and neighbor, and empowered by His grace demonstrate a faith that is alive and effective.

This navigational guide has attempted to guide reflection on how this principle applies to you personally. The challenge emerging from James is not to strive for works-based righteousness, but to allow the transforming power of genuine, saving faith – received by grace – to permeate every aspect of life. It is an invitation to cooperate with the Holy Spirit, becoming not just hearers of the Word, but consistent "doers," demonstrating the reality of God's work within through love, mercy, justice, patience, and integrity. I hope this guided portion of your journey encourages an ongoing pursuit of a faith that actively engages with the world, reflects the character of Christ, and brings glory to God.

The Navigator's Guide Series

Welcome to the Navigator's Guide series of introspective questions.

We don't pretend to have the answers for your life, we try to give you guided, intentional questions for you to discover how the Holy Spirit is leading you as an individual follower of Christ.

DISCLAIMER

The questions were generated using an AI prompt and edited by us.

A Pilocon LLC Publication
www.pilocon.com

This is a pre formal publication copy of this book.

Once we take the book to full publication there may be some changes.

Thanks for reviewing this copy and any feedback you can give us is greatly appreciated.

www.ingramcontent.com/pod-product-compliance
Lightning Source LLC
Chambersburg PA
CBHW081908110426
R18126300002B/R181263PG42743CBX00006B/1

9798999572400